promises

THE COLORS OF
GOD'S RAINBOW

PAULA MASTERS

Copyright ©2023 by Paula Masters

All rights reserved. This book or any portion thereof may not be reproduced or used in any manner whatsoever without the express written permission of the publisher except for the use of brief quotations in a book review.

ISBN Paperback: 978-1-7377427-5-3

ISBN Hardcover: 978-1-7377427-4-6

Published by Farmhouse Press

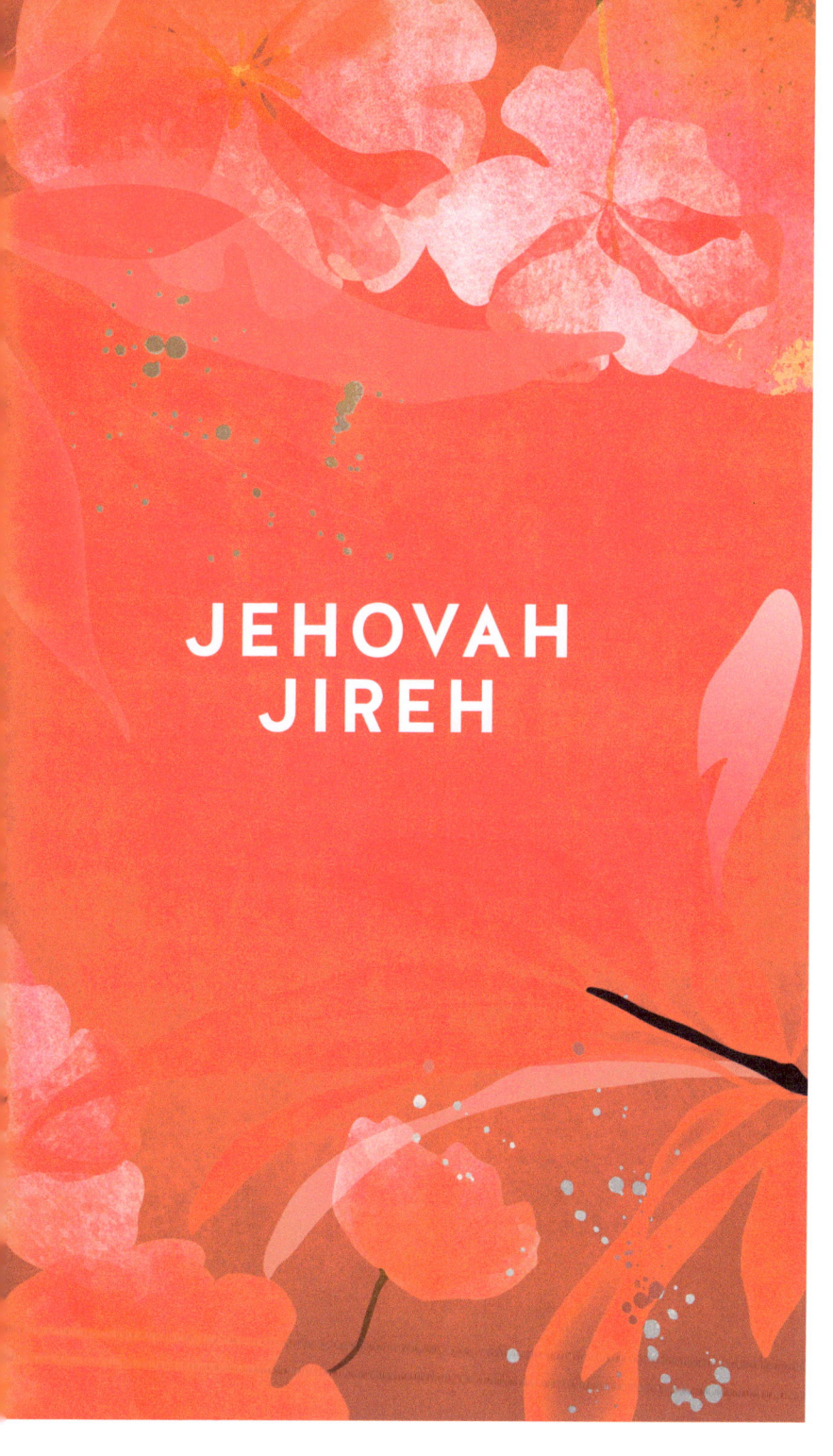

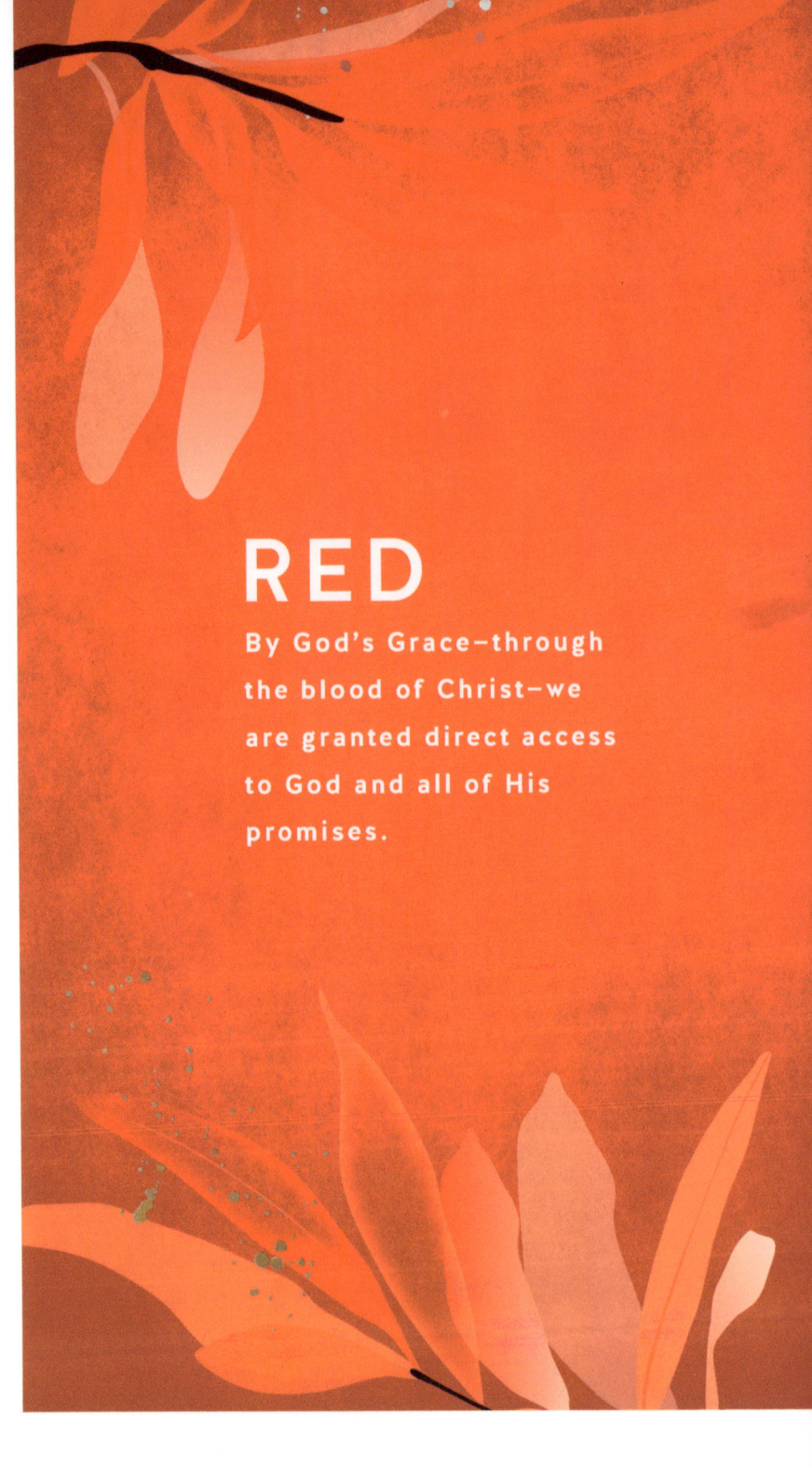

RED

By God's Grace—through the blood of Christ—we are granted direct access to God and all of His promises.

"We have confidence to enter the Most Holy Place by the blood of Jesus."

Hebrews 10:19

Red reminds us of the blood Christ shed to redeem our souls. God paints over our transgressions with the crimson-soaked brush of His atoning grace. This sacrifice is a stunning portrait of our covenant relationship—even making us heirs with Jesus. Because of His blood, the devil has absolutely no access to our souls. But without His blood, we have no personal connection to God at all. For this reason, it's important to remember that JEHOVAH JIREH—*The Lord Will Provide*—has made a way. Faith in His provision on the cross grants us full access to all of God's promises.

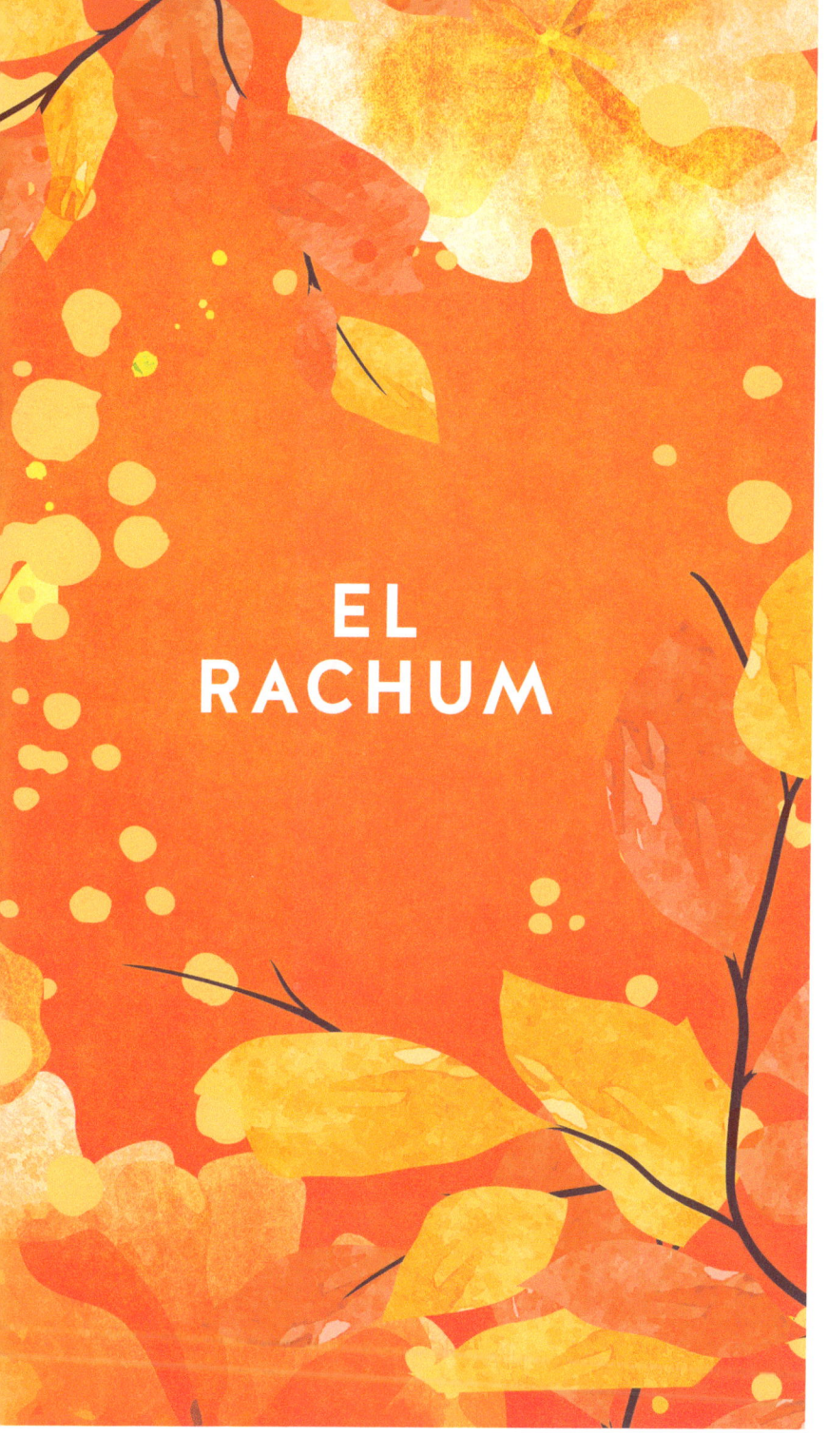

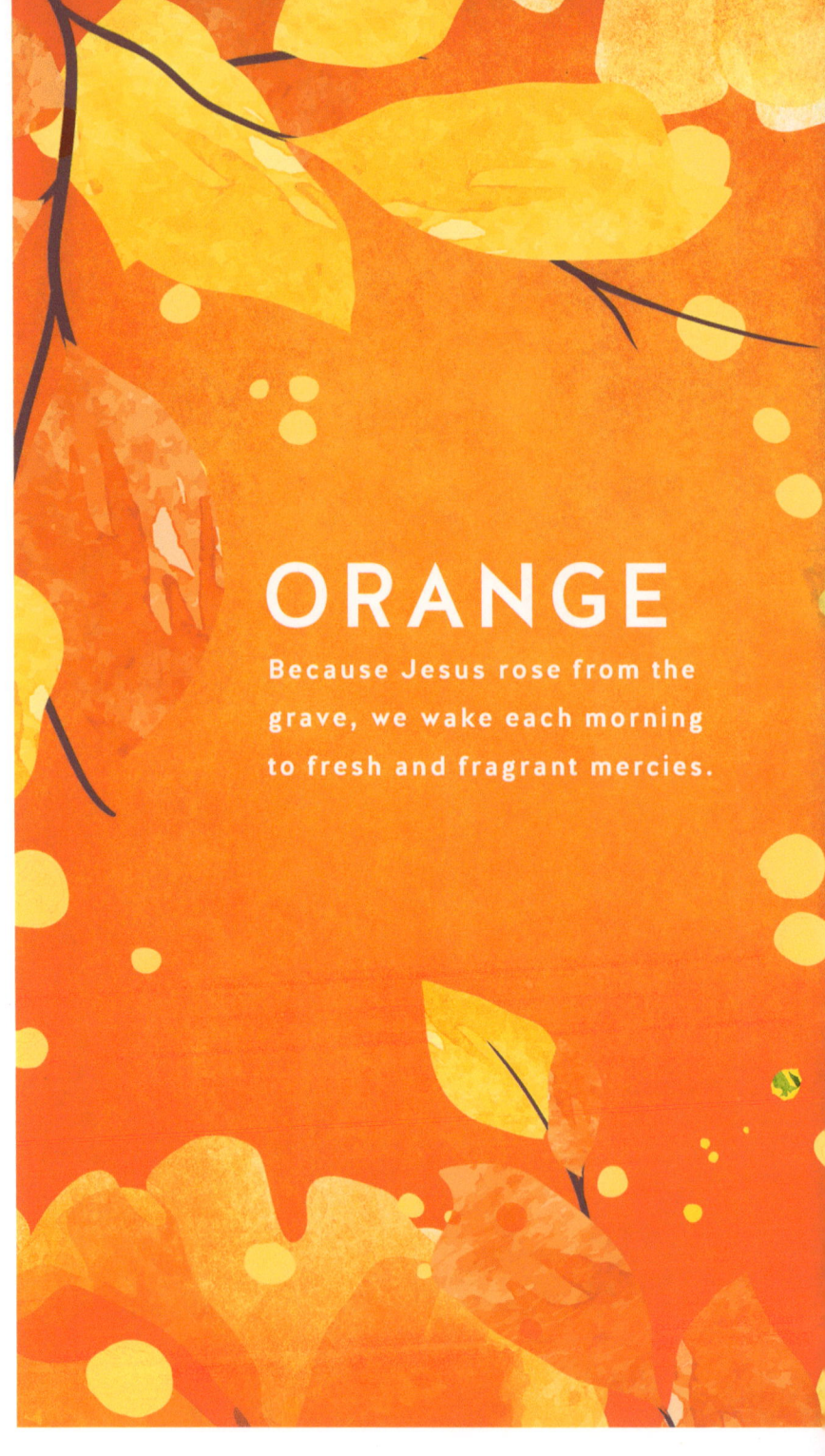

ORANGE

Because Jesus rose from the grave, we wake each morning to fresh and fragrant mercies.

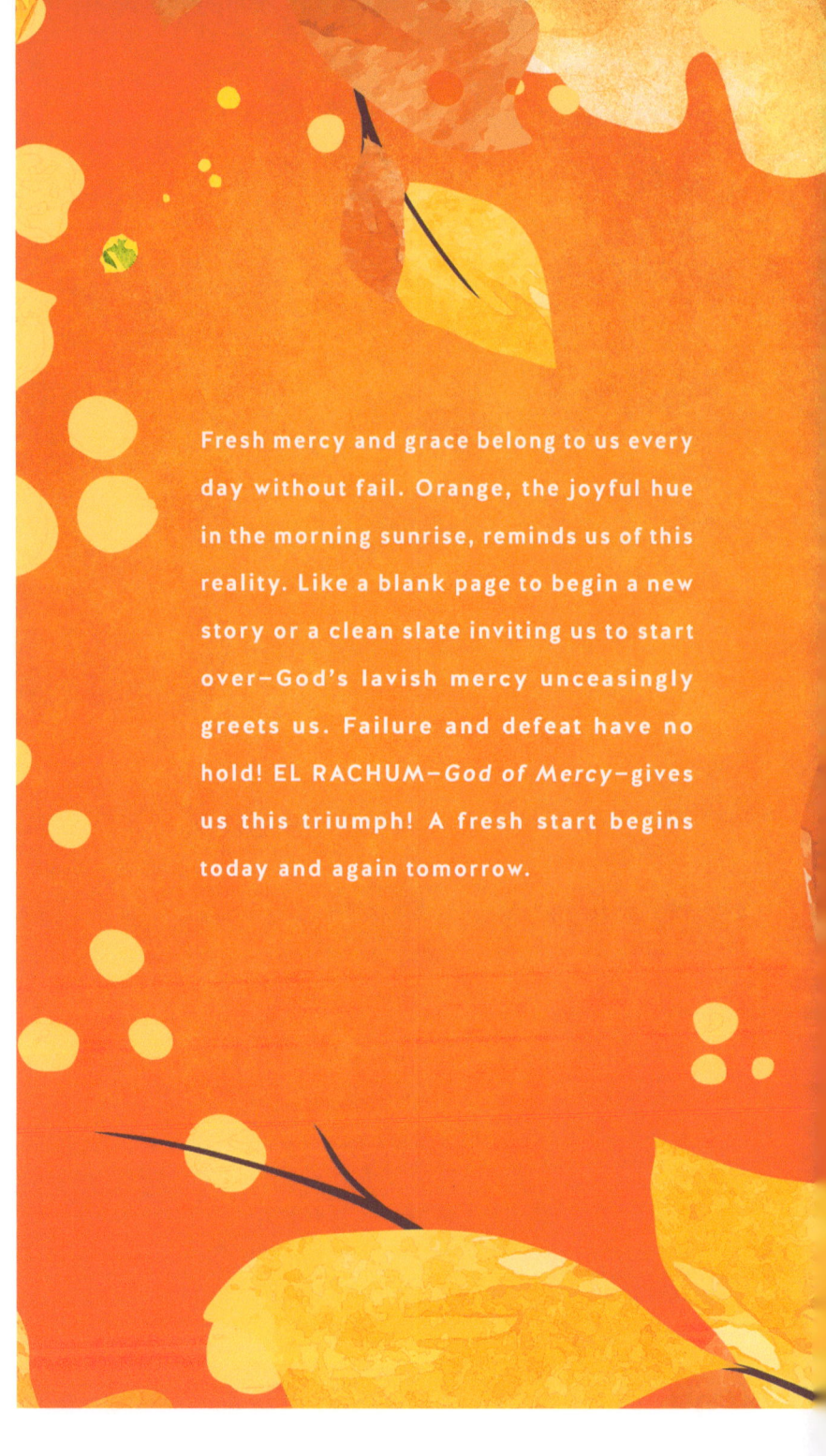

Fresh mercy and grace belong to us every day without fail. Orange, the joyful hue in the morning sunrise, reminds us of this reality. Like a blank page to begin a new story or a clean slate inviting us to start over—God's lavish mercy unceasingly greets us. Failure and defeat have no hold! EL RACHUM—*God of Mercy*—gives us this triumph! A fresh start begins today and again tomorrow.

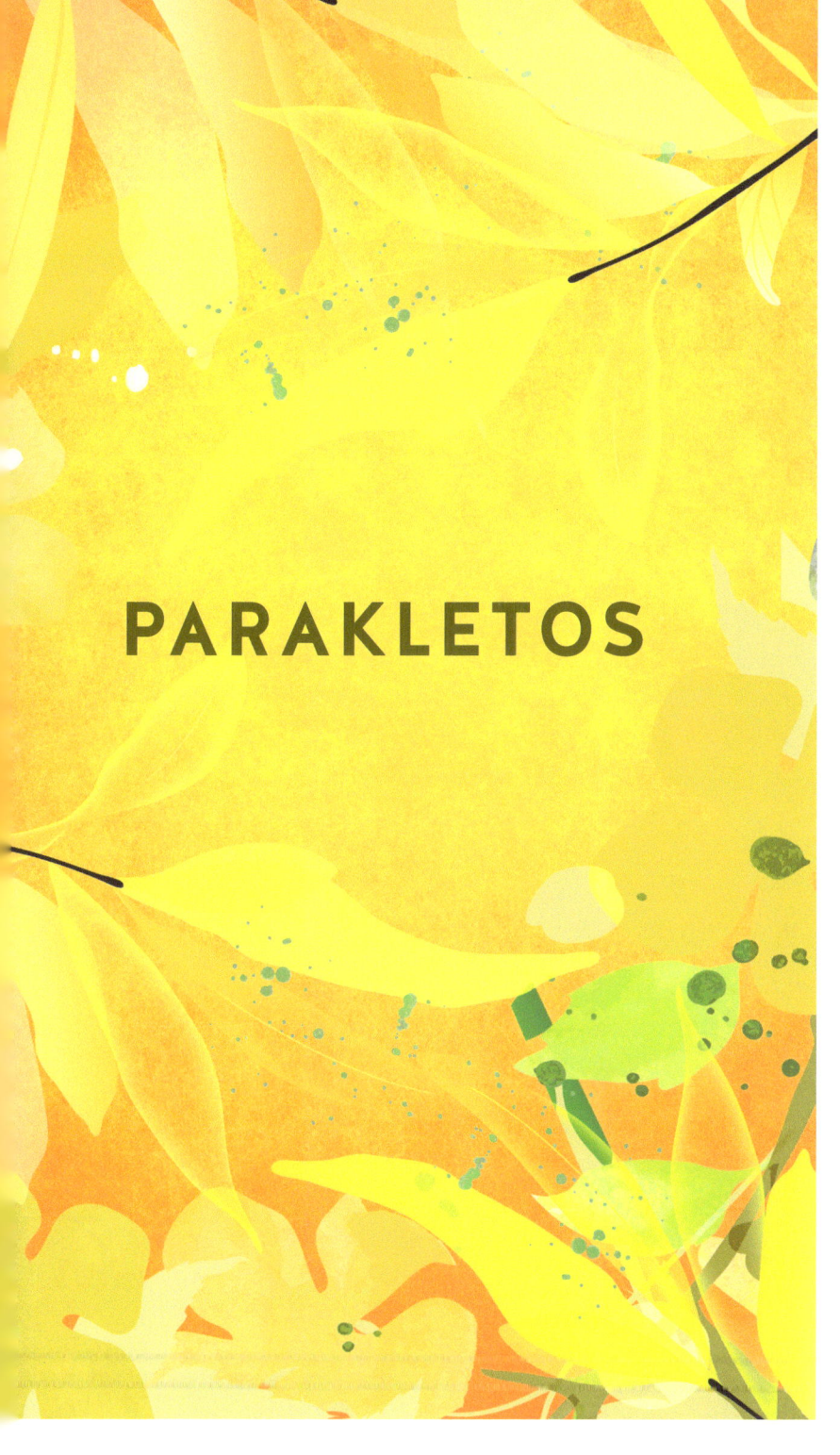

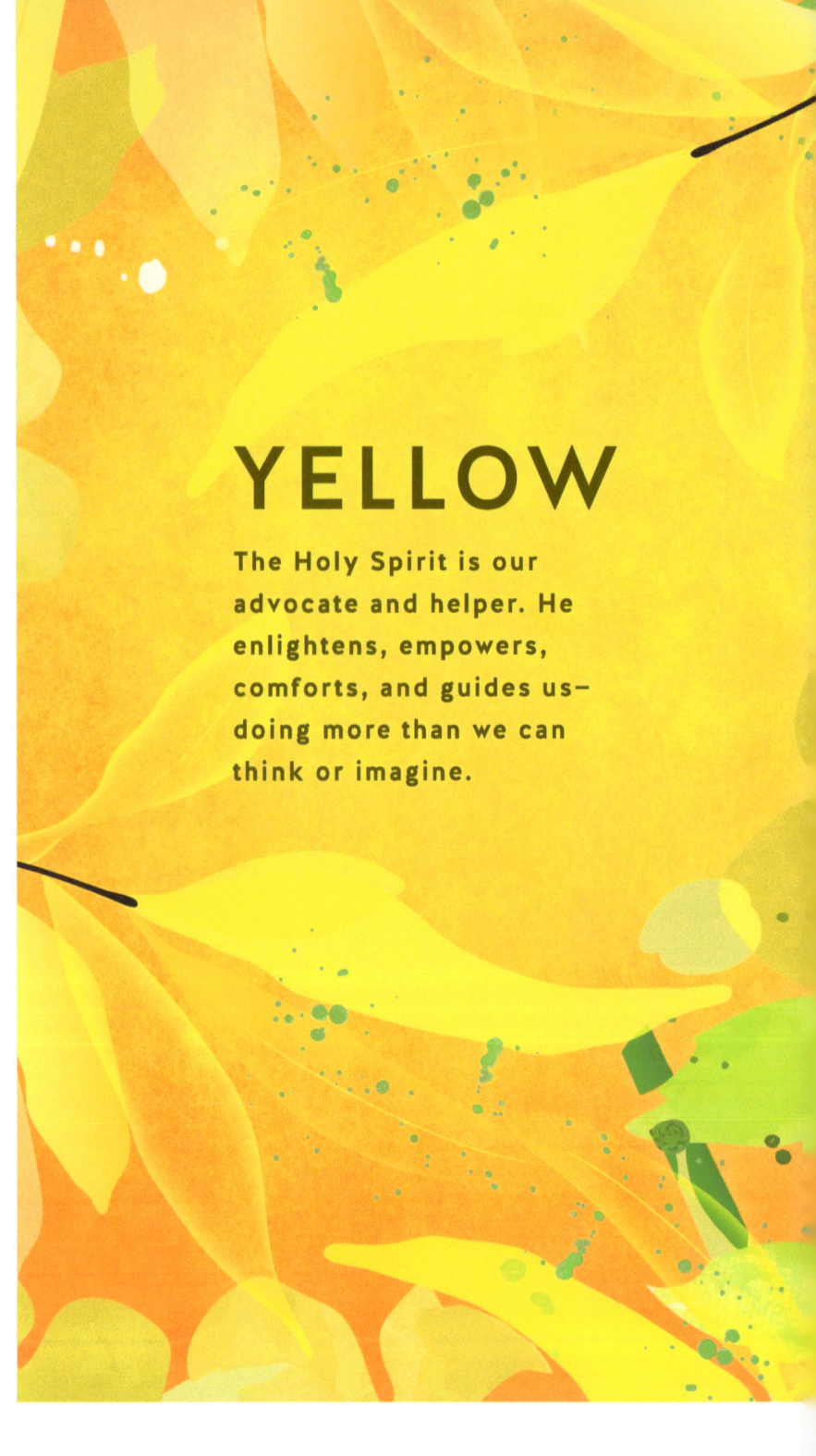

YELLOW

The Holy Spirit is our advocate and helper. He enlightens, empowers, comforts, and guides us—doing more than we can think or imagine.

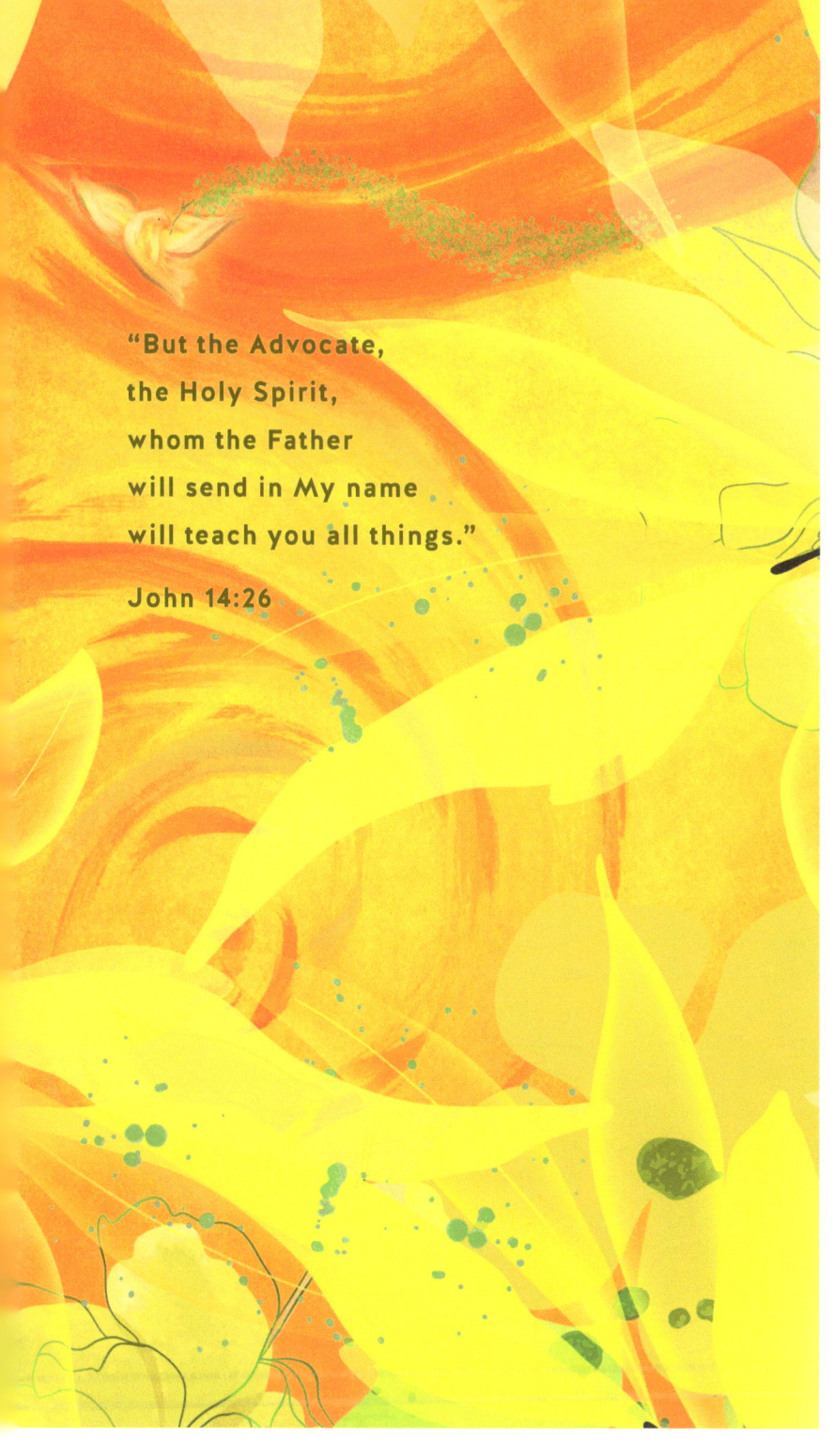

"But the Advocate,
the Holy Spirit,
whom the Father
will send in My name
will teach you all things."

John 14:26

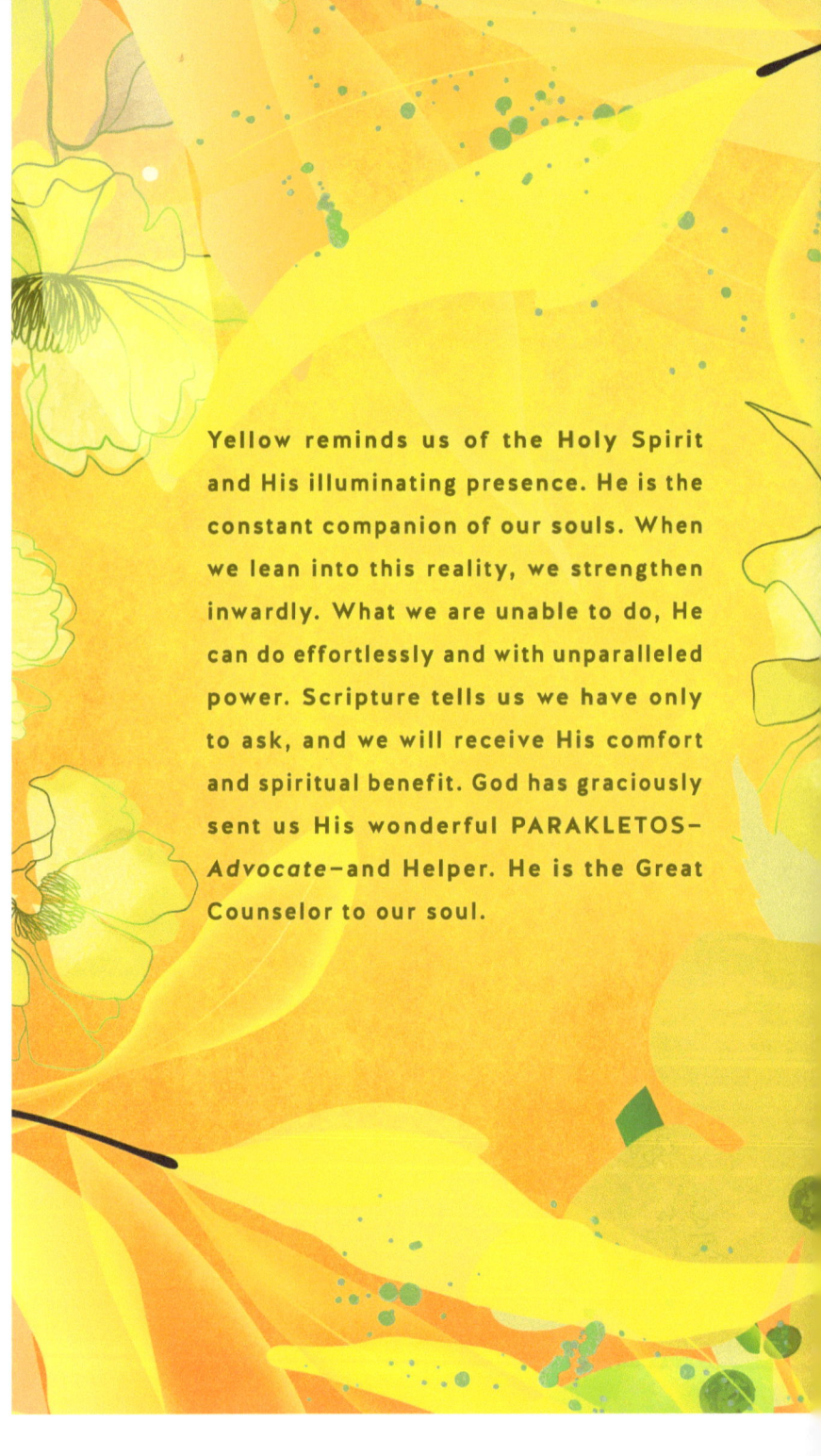

Yellow reminds us of the Holy Spirit and His illuminating presence. He is the constant companion of our souls. When we lean into this reality, we strengthen inwardly. What we are unable to do, He can do effortlessly and with unparalleled power. Scripture tells us we have only to ask, and we will receive His comfort and spiritual benefit. God has graciously sent us His wonderful PARAKLETOS–*Advocate*–and Helper. He is the Great Counselor to our soul.

GREEN

All growth and renewal come from God, who creates in us a flourishing Eden. He tends to our hearts as a garden, working everything (even the bad) together for good.

"God, who began a good work within you, will continue His work until it is finally finished on the day when Christ Jesus returns."

Philippians 1:6

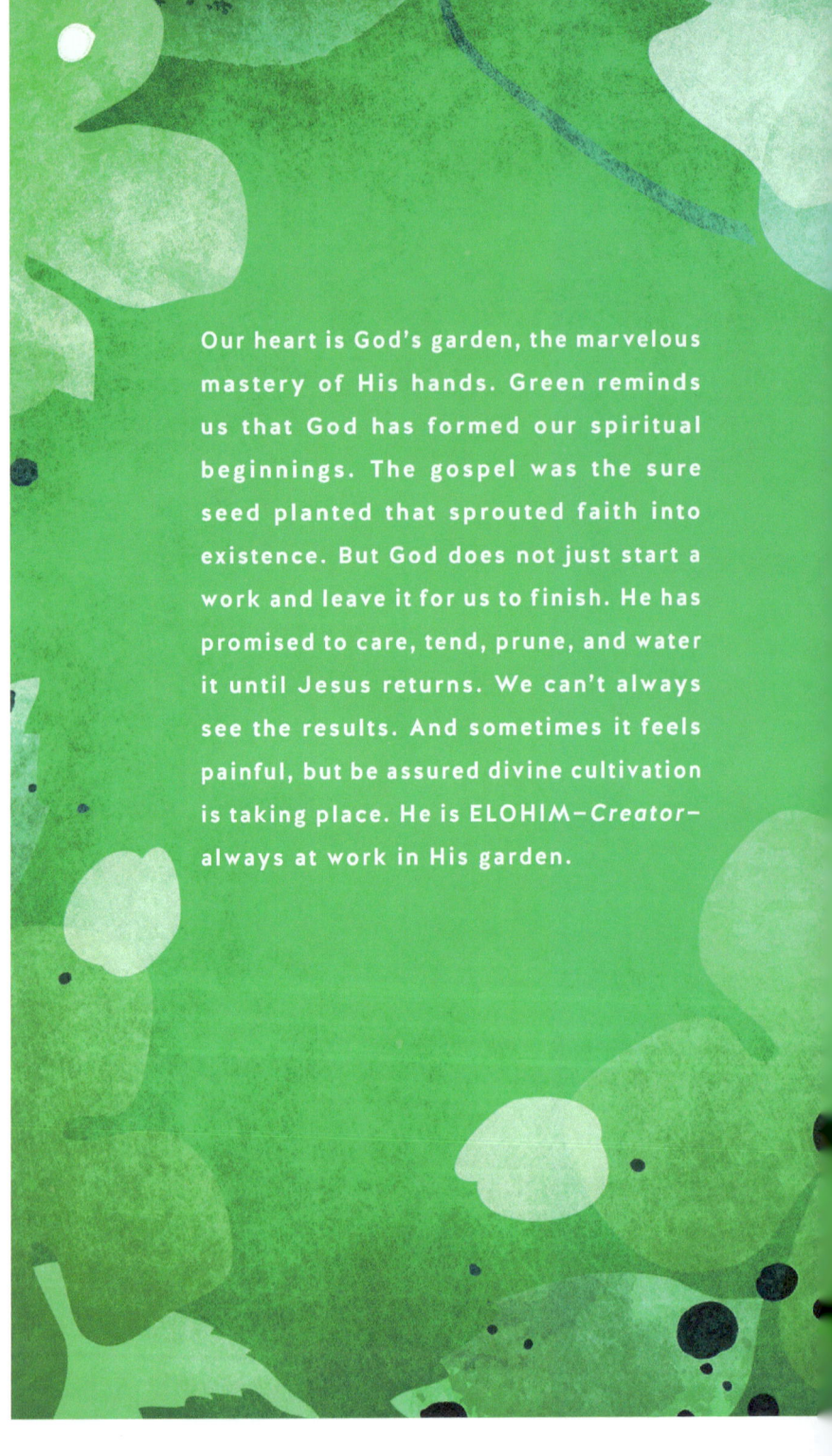

Our heart is God's garden, the marvelous mastery of His hands. Green reminds us that God has formed our spiritual beginnings. The gospel was the sure seed planted that sprouted faith into existence. But God does not just start a work and leave it for us to finish. He has promised to care, tend, prune, and water it until Jesus returns. We can't always see the results. And sometimes it feels painful, but be assured divine cultivation is taking place. He is ELOHIM—*Creator*—always at work in His garden.

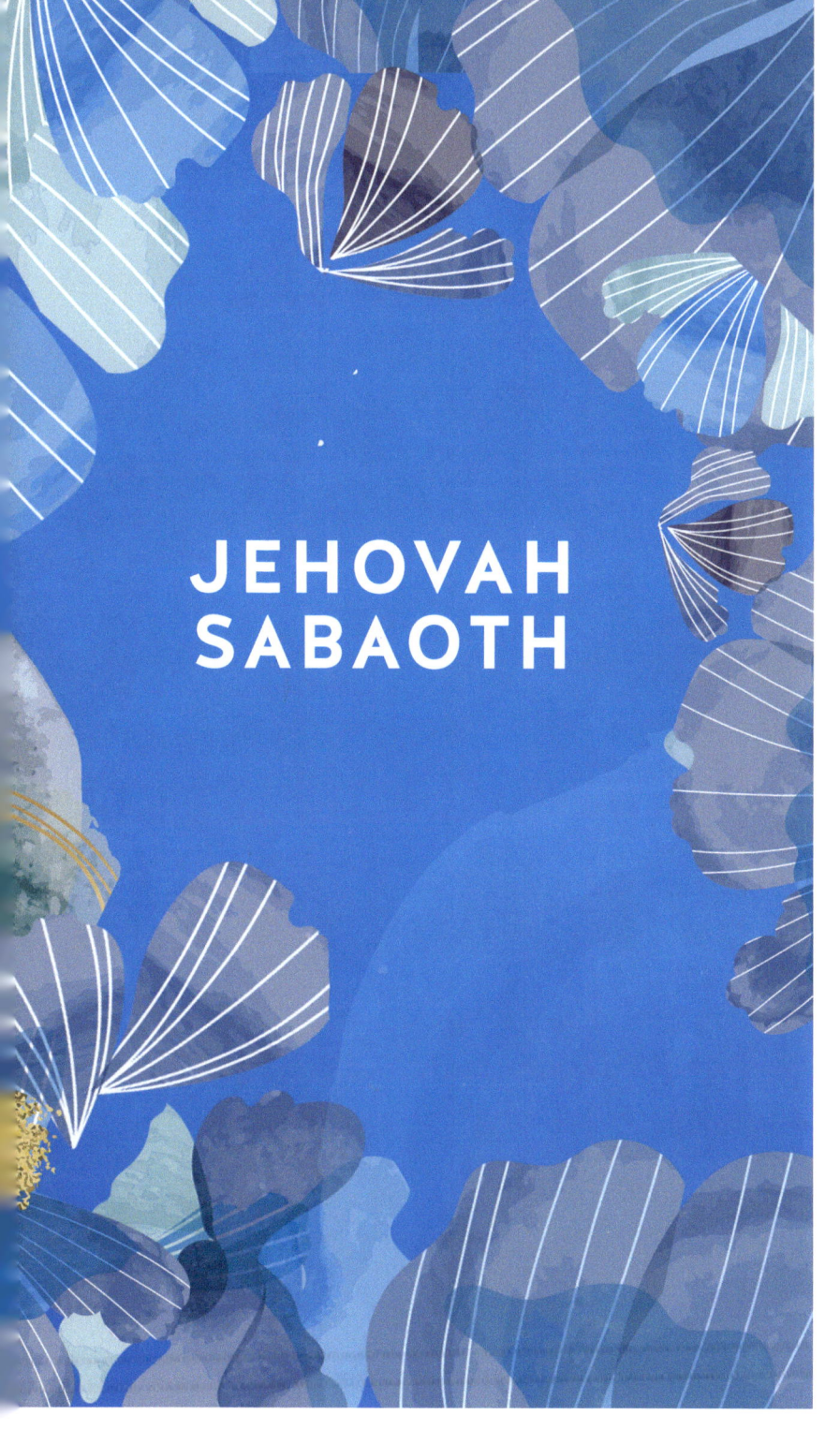

BLUE

A heavenly kingdom sparkles and shines all around us, and even though we don't see it—we belong to its grander purpose. Someday, our eyes will open to its stunning fullness.

Blue reminds us that we belong to a spiritual kingdom where the Lord reigns supreme. Scripture assures us of this unseen reality—angels among us celebrating the ongoing work of God. Life often feels temporary and without purpose—until we remember God rules over all things—the seen and the unseen—including dominions past, present, and future. We are part of this grand assembly! He is JEHOVAH SABAOTH—*Lord of Hosts*—the King of all heaven and earth.

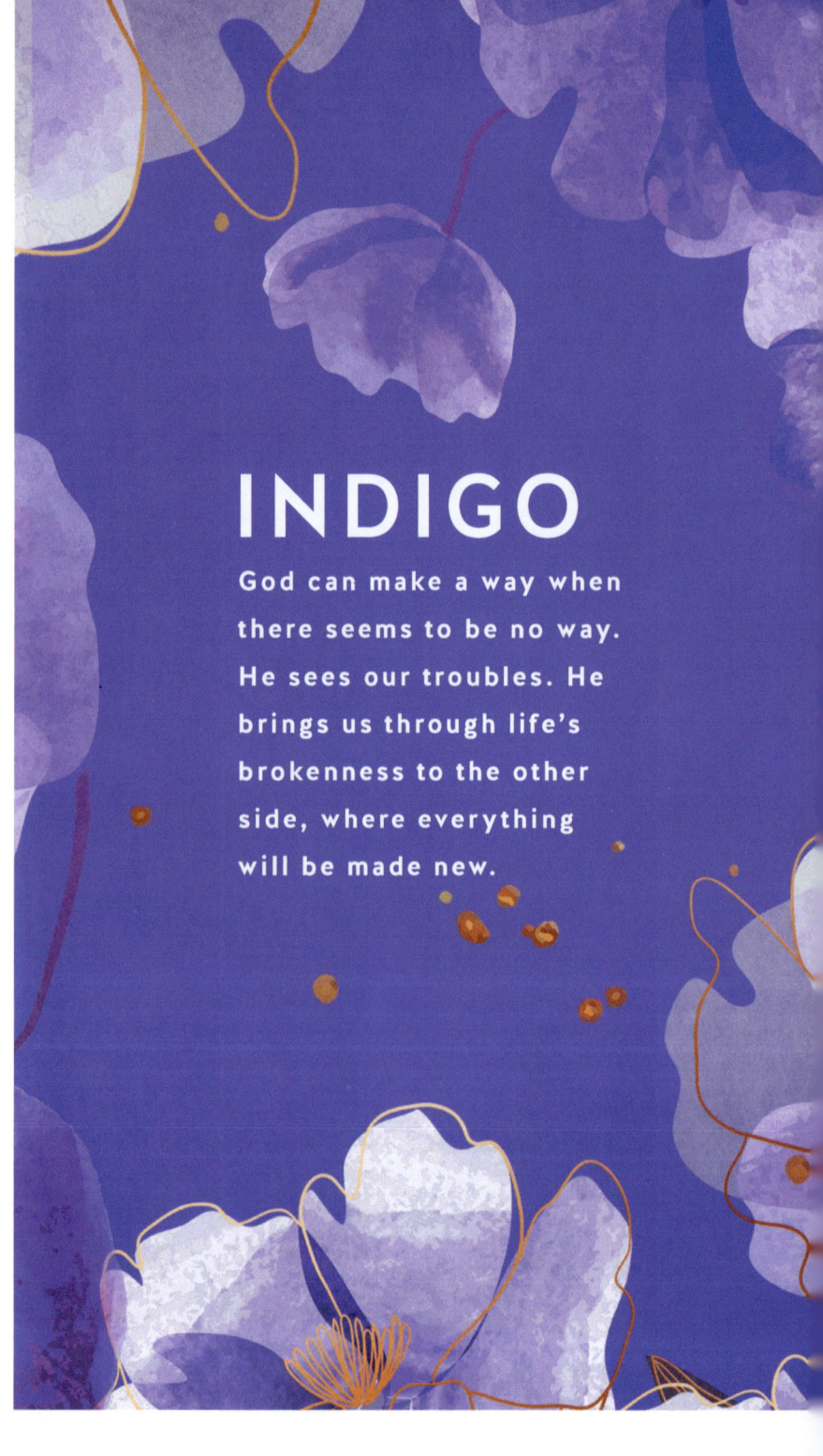

INDIGO

God can make a way when there seems to be no way. He sees our troubles. He brings us through life's brokenness to the other side, where everything will be made new.

"Are You not the same today, the One who dried up the sea, making a path of escape through the depths so Your people might cross over?"

Isaiah 51:10

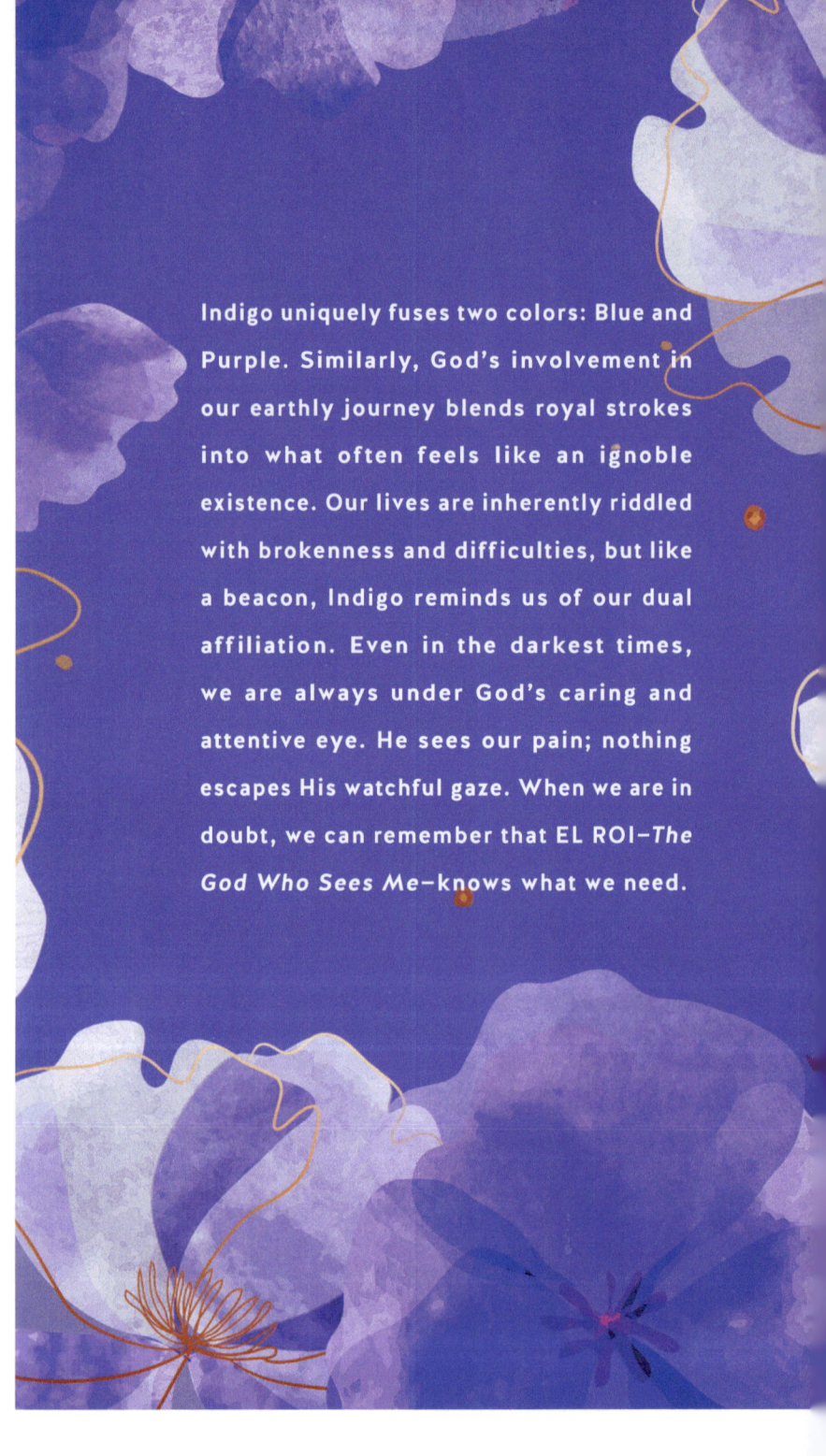

Indigo uniquely fuses two colors: Blue and Purple. Similarly, God's involvement in our earthly journey blends royal strokes into what often feels like an ignoble existence. Our lives are inherently riddled with brokenness and difficulties, but like a beacon, Indigo reminds us of our dual affiliation. Even in the darkest times, we are always under God's caring and attentive eye. He sees our pain; nothing escapes His watchful gaze. When we are in doubt, we can remember that EL ROI—*The God Who Sees Me*—knows what we need.

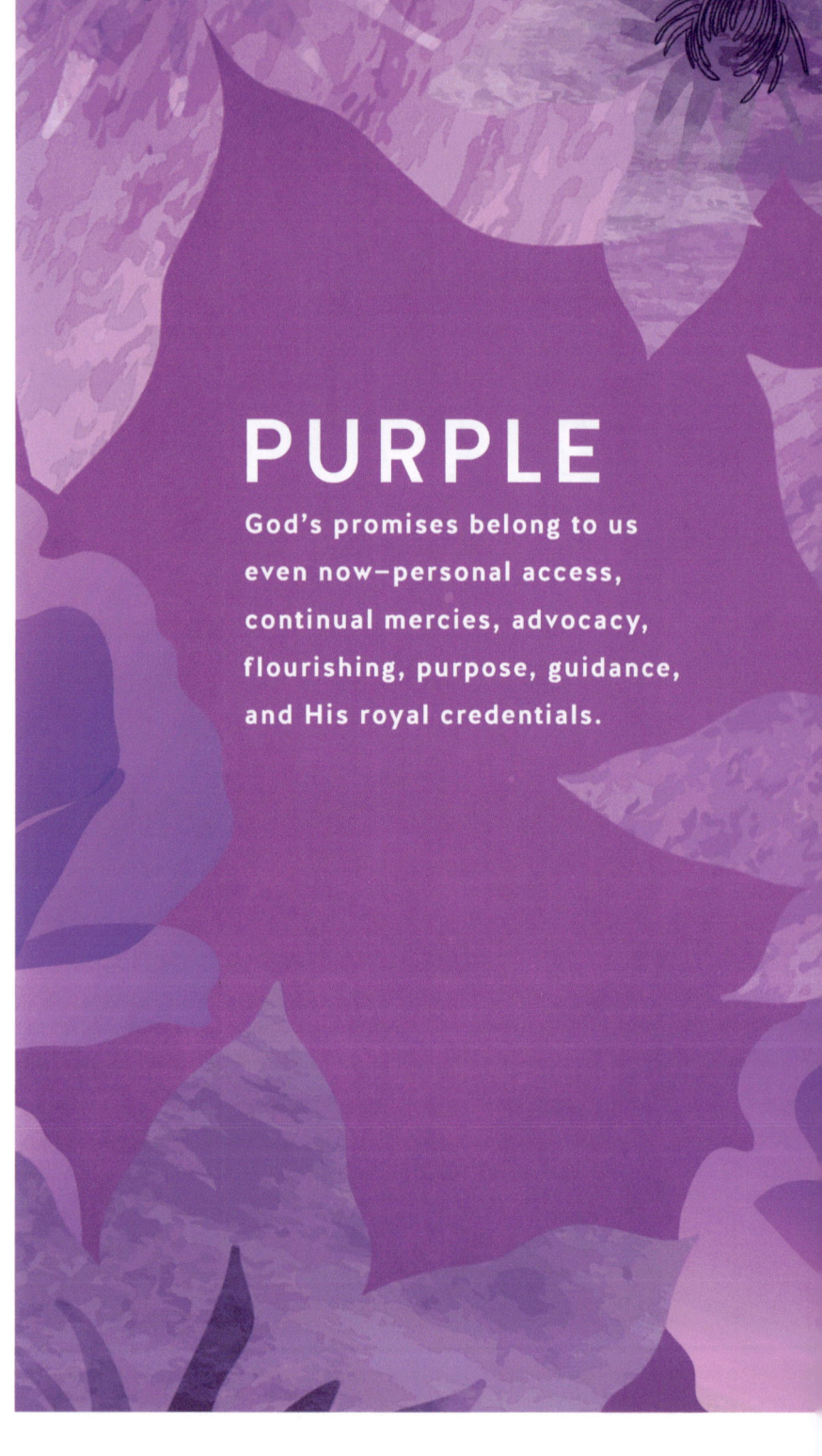

PURPLE

God's promises belong to us even now—personal access, continual mercies, advocacy, flourishing, purpose, guidance, and His royal credentials.

"You are a chosen people, a holy priesthood, a holy nation, God's special possession, that you may declare the praises of Him who called you out of the darkness into His wonderful light."

1 Peter 2:9

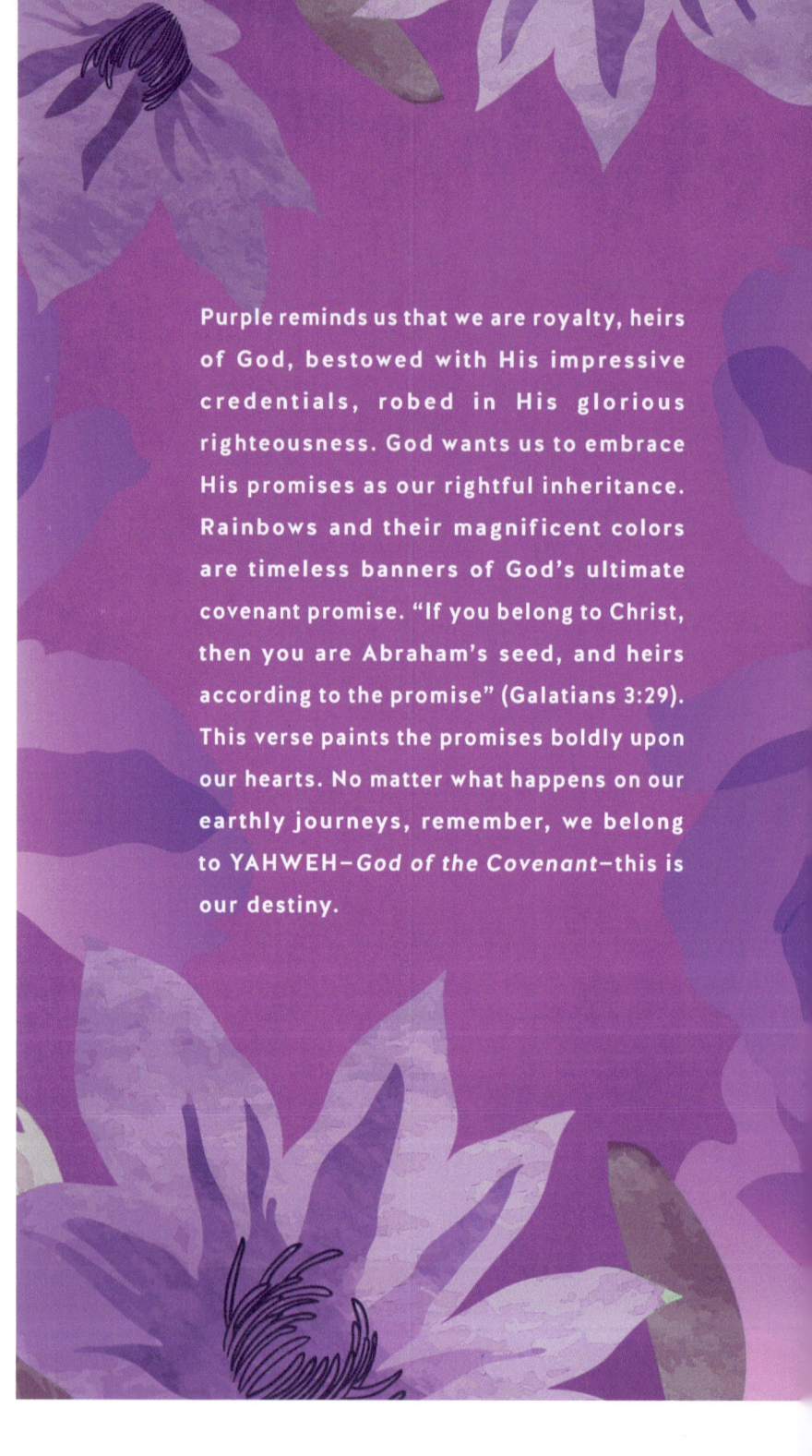

Purple reminds us that we are royalty, heirs of God, bestowed with His impressive credentials, robed in His glorious righteousness. God wants us to embrace His promises as our rightful inheritance. Rainbows and their magnificent colors are timeless banners of God's ultimate covenant promise. "If you belong to Christ, then you are Abraham's seed, and heirs according to the promise" (Galatians 3:29). This verse paints the promises boldly upon our hearts. No matter what happens on our earthly journeys, remember, we belong to YAHWEH–*God of the Covenant*–this is our destiny.

JEHOVAH JIREH
The Lord Will Provide

EL RACHUM
God of Mercy

PARAKLETOS
Advocate

ELOHIM
Creator

JEHOVAH SABAOTH
Lord of Hosts

EL ROI
The God Who Sees Me

YAHWEH
God of the Covenant

www.ingramcontent.com/pod-product-compliance
Lightning Source LLC
Chambersburg PA
CBHW042202170426
43209CB00047BA/1723

Your baby is ugly.

For Shanda, Taylin, and Dakota,
none of whom have ever had an ugly baby!!

(...yet)

Your baby is ugly.
Text and illustrations copyright © 2021 by Maren Jones
All rights reserved.

Published by Happy Happy Living
https://www.happyhappyliving.com
For information about permission to reproduce selections
from this book, write to Permissions, Happy Happy Living
1594 E. Grand Canyon Drive, Chandler, AZ 85249.

First printing edition 2021.

10 9 8 7 6 5 4 3 2 1

ISBN: 978-1-7368723-4-5 (paperback)
ISBN: 978-1-7368723-5-2 (ebook)
ISBN: 978-1-7368723-3-8 (hardback)

Your baby is ugly.

Maren Jones

A HAPPY·HAPPY·LIVING™ book

When you've got a baby, some people (NOT ME!) might say insensitive things like...

"Your baby is ugly."

> Babies are always covered in poop and barf and disgusting slime.

I sort of resent that last part.

Aw, I think your baby is cute!

Um, sorry.

Look at those chubby cheeks! I could just gobble them up!

(Translation: I want to eat your baby.)

> Your baby should only come out at night.

> Congratulations!
> It's a gorilla!
>
> Er, I mean,
> it's a GIRL!

Your baby could scare away the crows in my cornfield.

Of course,
lots of people say
very kind things
about babies.

(...but some of them are lying!)

Just remember, when it's YOUR baby, the only opinion that really matters is YOURS.

www.ingramcontent.com/pod-product-compliance
Lightning Source LLC
Chambersburg PA
CBHW042202170426
43209CB00047BA/1725